OVER HONG KONG

Pearl River Delta Taken from a Landsat satellite, Hong Kong is at lower right, and Canton, China, is in the centre (courtesy of NASA, No. 8152002210500)

OVER HONG KONG

Photographs by Magnus Bartlett
with Lew Roberts

Preface by
Sir David Akers-Jones

Introduction by David Bonavia

Odyssey Productions Limited

OVER HONG KONG VOLUME TWO

© Copyright Odyssey Productions Ltd., 1987

Photography © Airphoto International Ltd.

First Impression, November 1987
Second edition. 1988
ISBN 962-217-031-5

Published by Odyssey Productions Ltd.
The Penthouse, No. 20, Hollywood Road
Central, Hong Kong.
Fax: 5-8450774 Telex: 61714 CGSL HX
Printed by Mandarin Offset, Hong Kong

Captions by Lesley Hargreaves and Peter Fry
Additional photography by Robbie Shaw and Richard Strong
Colour Separations by Sakai Lithocolour
Design and Artwork by Joan Law Design and Photography

CONTENTS

Right
Lamma Fields On Hong Kong's outlying islands, along with parts of the New Territories, a traditional and often agriculture-based way of life still prevails. Small farmers on Lamma Island tend these fields of vegetables the time-honoured way, which includes irrigating, fertilizing and harvesting their crops by hand. Another member of the family will usually carry them to market.

Above
Mai Po At Mai Po the crops are very different. This protected marshland in the New Territories is a series of shrimp and fish ponds well known for its varied wildlife.

Top
Fairview Park Next door to Mai Po on the northwest coast of the New Territories, this residential development offers the luxury of low-rise living in a rural environment.

Bottom
Yuen Long Fields The rolling hills and fields of Yuen Long, Hong Kong's most important agricultural area, are seen in sharp contrast here with the massive development of Shenzhen in China.

Central District Construction never stops in Hong Kong's busy Central District, the business and commercial hub of the territory. Featured here are the since completed Bond Centre, the spectacular twin towers soaring up behind the bronze Far East Finance Centre at centre. Next to them and also still under construction, are the new headquarters for the Bank of China which, when complete, will become the world's tallest building outside America. Another recent addition to the cityscape are the Queensway government offices rising solidly to the left.

Helicopter over Star Ferry This machine, flown by Captain Doug Cavannagh, is the AS 350B Ecureuil, made by Aerospatiale of France. Its single engine lifts a machine weighing 2,432 pounds, achieves a fuel economy of just over two nautical miles per gallon, and rotates its three main blades 386 times each minute. Photographer Magnus Bartlett is using the large format 6x7 Pentax, a rugged camera ideal for this kind of work. The majority of pictures in the book were shot on Fujichrome Professional film, type 50D. Shutter speed was usually 1/500 of a second although the dusk shots of the Jumbo Floating Restaurant (P.55) and Tsim Sha Tsui (P.68) were made at a slow 1/30th with aperture wide open and forced processing of film — hence the grainy images. (Photographed by Richard Strong)

A PREFACE TO HONG KONG

by Sir David Akers-Jones

The photographs in this book let the fleeting visitor, the long time resident and those who have not had the good fortune to visit Hong Kong, fly for a brief while over the skyscrapers, the busy streets, the clustered ships, to swim in the imagination on silver-sanded beaches, to stand on rugged cliffs and to want to climb the wind-swept grass of the hills and mountains of Hong Kong.

Hong Kong (香 港) — fragrant harbour — grew into the great city it is today because of its harbour. It gave shelter to sailing ships from the West one hundred and fifty years ago, and is still today visited by tens of thousands of vessels each year. So it is that the composition of many photographs in this book is held together by the waters of the harbour or the waters that wash the cliffs of the several hundred islands which dot the sea around Hong Kong.

There can be no definitive book of photographs of Hong Kong: its skyline, after only a few years, is changed. In the centre of the city little now remains of the old arcades and covered walkways; the flags of shipping lines no longer flutter along the waterfront. Glass walls gleam in the sun, and in their glittering faces reflect tomorrow's world of instant communication and high finance.

Piled high container boxes like toys wait for the eager ships which slip quietly in and quietly out. Foam follows the fast ferries to Macau and up the Pearl River to Canton; and slowly through the harbour occasionally still, with leaning masts, patched brown-washed sails, a junk slips by imperturbably.

Hong Kong — a home and homes for so many people. Fewer now in flimsy huts cling to crowded corners and impossible slopes; fewer now the fires, floods and landslides. Tower blocks, in tridents and quadrangles and webs of concrete, now more tidily contain the tens of thousands of families whose work and industry makes the city alive with ceaseless movement and whose homes light up the night with countless stars.

Streets with pale jade bracelets sold on the side walks; a street, closed to cars, full of cheap clothes for thrifty housewives; streets of birds and goldfish; streets of rice, tea, medicinal herbs, antiques for the unwary; cameras, radios, calculators in endless variety; colour and confusion of sounds and people ceaselessly hurrying: this is Hong Kong.

Tower blocks like pale needles catch the light under grey clouds, the yellow roof of a monastery catches the sun, mist hangs above and below the mountain tops as though commanded by the artist's brush. Hong Kong is not just all crowds and concrete, beyond the hills that hem the harbour in are empty landscapes, hidden valleys, dark woods and deserted villages, and farms to feed the city: plenty of places to get away from it all.

It is a place of movement and change, but behind the facade and the hurrying faces, people hold on to custom and tradition. Incense burns by the roadside, processions wend their way from villages past towering concrete to find the temple; and, while the pumps of the village fire brigade and a dragon head gather dust, the dragon boats race now more fiercely and numerous than ever before; and opera has found its way from the village yard into the concert hall.

This year begins another cycle in the Chinese tradition: a cycle of sixty years. Sixty years ago Hong Kong was a trading port of a few hundred thousand people, small in comparison to Shanghai. In ten years time China will resume her sovereignty, but Hong Kong, its life-style and its systems, will stay for another fifty years. After that, 2047 will mark the end of another cycle.

Throughout its relatively short history people have come to Hong Kong to trade, to live and to work. It has no resources except its people and its harbour and, while not a nation itself, this tiny place now ranks thirteenth among the trading nations of the world.

Apart from brief interruptions, Hong Kong has enjoyed long periods of stability and has made the most of this advantage to build up a living standard that is among the highest in Asia, allowing it to enjoy long periods of sustained prosperity. This makes for a lively community but fewer sensational headlines than most cities of comparable size.

Hong Kong is a Chinese city: Chinese from all parts of China but speaking Cantonese as a common tongue. It is Chinese and cosmopolitan: people from all over the world mingle in the streets using English as a lingua franca.

It is trade — nineteenth century trade with all its overtones of imperialism, its aggressions and its seamy side, its heroisms and its cruelties; and twentieth century trade with its jumbo jets, giant ships and great buildings — and it is people that have made Hong Kong a great city of the world, a modern miracle.

With the resumption of Chinese sovereignty in 1997 Hong Kong faces another exciting chapter in its history. It faces it with realism, knowing that all the ingredients which have contributed to its prosperity in the past will be retained, but conscious that nothing quite like this transfer of sovereignty has ever happened before. But Hong Kong has accepted and overcome many challenges in its past and will do so in the future.

INTRODUCTION

by David Bonavia

I must confess to being something of a Hong Kong nut. I fell in love with the place the moment I set eyes on it in 1964. I know what the detractors say, and I admit that there are certain unattractive features about Hong Kong to which one simply cannot close one's eyes. But these moans are usually voiced by expatriates who can always move somewhere else if they really want; I am thinking of the six million local Chinese who have nowhere else to go and tend to look at Hong Kong through more familiar and realistic eyes.

Criticism is all too easy: the heat and humidity, the noise and overcrowding, pollution, crime and vice — all part of daily life in Hong Kong, but then again so is that the case for Naples or Rio de Janeiro or a number of other places I could mention. It is carping on points like this that brings home the sad fact that the actual beauty of Hong Kong is often masked from those bustling at ground level by the problems of a modern urban society going through the necessary growing pains.

Hong Kong with all its joys and trials will not simply fade away on being declared constitutionally part of the People's Republic of China in 1997. All the factories, beaches and universities will still be very much in evidence and, in fact, it is these aerial views of the territory that bring home the sheer modernity of the place and those very principles of planning that one is sometimes tempted to believe hardly exist.

Like some lady of easy virtue basking in her own slightly racy reputation, the territory takes each day as it comes, but with the sort of easy self-acceptance on the part of most of its people that still admits its more tarnished features.

Hong Kong divides roughly into a number of areas but officially it comprises Hong Kong Island, Kowloon and the New Territories. The island itself falls yet further into various divisions: the business district of Victoria Central that is rapidly encroaching on the restaurant district of Wanchai; the Causeway Bay shopping paradise on the northeastern shore; the Happy Valley middle-class residential area around the race track; the new industrial towns of Quarry Bay and Shaukeiwan; and the beaches and resort developments along the island's south coast together with the fishing port of Aberdeen, still recognisable amidst the factory complexes, and where a boat trip around the typhoon shelter never fails to interest.

Across the harbour on the mainland is the Kowloon shopping and business centre of Tsim Sha Tsui (literally 'Sharp Beak of Land') which soon gives way to the New Territories townships such as Kwun Tong and Tsuen Wan which make up the local manufacturing and industrial areas from which pour the innumerable goods for export. And, of course, there are the nearly 240 islands, most of them tiny and uninhabited, but also including the largest and most picturesque such as Lantau with its Buddhist monastery, Cheung Chau and its quaint religious festivals, and Lamma off Hong Kong Island's south coast with its popular seafood restaurants. Further along, to the southwest, there is Ap Lei Chau (or 'Duck's Tongue Island' because of its shape) which lies adjacent to Aberdeen and houses a power-generating station and shipyards making fishing junks.

Preceding page
Aberdeen With the Aberdeen Marina, the Jumbo floating restaurant and the new fishing junks being built at lower centre, Aberdeen Harbour is home to much lively activity, including the yearly dragon boat races. Long before the British arrived, Aberdeen was known for its piracy as well as its fishing. Today, factories and new housing developments dominate the scene, including the Ap Lei Chau Estates rising at right on the island of the same name. Beyond the harbour can be seen Ocean Park and Repulse Bay.

Left
Hong Kong through a Fisheye With Government House at lower centre just above the residential towers of the Mid-Levels, and straight below Exchange Square and the Connaught Centre, this photograph was taken with a Takumar 35mm Fisheye lens on a Pentax 6x7 camera-body. The dark shadows on the water reflect the scattered clouds above on what was an otherwise perfect day for shooting aerial pictures.

Left
Tsim Sha Tsui The incredible diversity of Hong Kong's architecture is very evident in this overview of the Kowloon Peninsula and Hong Kong Island beyond. The unusual inverted pyramid of the Hong Kong Coliseum occupies the foreground with, to its right, the utilitarian terminus for the Kowloon-Canton Railway. Sweeping along the eastern waterfront are the relatively new luxury hotels and shopping complexes of Tsim Sha Tsui East while the crowded tenement style buildings of old Tsim Sha Tsui occupy the background.

Above
Kwai Chung Container Port All the container yards and freight stations at Kwai Chung are operated by private companies and consortia in aggressively free-enterprise Hong Kong, although the public sector also maintains several cargo working facilities throughout the territory predominantly for the handling of internal shipments. The bridge in the background links Kwai Chung with the industrial zone of Tsing Yi Island across the Rambler Channel.

A bird's eye view of Hong Kong brings home the image of a modern city facing up to the rigorous problems of limited space made further difficult by a steep and rocky terrain. Evidence of this can be seen in the large Government-built water reservoir which, together with water piped in from China, has helped alleviate the recurrent water shortages. In fact, it is in the catchment areas of those reservoirs actually open to the public that ramblers and nature lovers come to enjoy some of the most spectacular countryside and spend an enjoyable weekend hiking or climbing.

Hong Kong's chief asset is its harbour, and its fortunes have been shaped by the waters that surround it. Small wonder then that one of the favourite pastimes of its wealthier residents centres on water sports and leisurely picnics in secluded coves and inlets. In fact, some expatriate boat-owners spend so much time on their craft that they are no doubt the envy of their friends and relatives back home for the ease and convenience with which they set sail, albeit on the increasingly polluted waters of the South China Sea.

The sea is Hong Kong's lifeblood, not just for the fishing but for the massive trading that goes on and which can be seen in the increasing number of goods being shipped by container from the impressive docks at Kwai Chung, adjacent to the Kowloon Peninsula. At the same time high-fashion goods and other expensive light products are also sent out by air freight, which is how Hong Kong in turn brings in its astonishing range of foreign foods and drink as well as the ever-widening range of costly designer-label items so popular with the increasingly prosperous 'locals'.

The most dignified reminder of Hong Kong's colonial past is Government House, the residence of the British Governor, a Foreign Office appointee whose duties include the important one of ensuring that relations with China maintain an even keel. With its shaven lawns and oriental-style tower (built by the Japanese occupation force during World War II), GH — as it is affectionately known to the British population — gleams from the hillside above Central like a huge white clam-shell from behind its screen of palm trees.

Below Government House the major banks and trading companies loom over Statue Square with its cenotaph and, next to it, stands the new Hong Kong Club building whose self-importance is almost at odds with its eccentric design that gives it the air of a somewhat outlandish multi-copying machine.

The oldest of the senior financial institutions, the Hongkong Bank (previously known as the Hongkong and Shanghai Banking Corporation), has been newly housed in a huge and futuristic building of admirable stylistic daring which some people love, others hate and some even refer to jokingly as a monstrous space-rocket in thin disguise.

Other mammoth constructions are going up along that western stretch of the waterfront previously known by the Portuguese word *praya* and these are encroaching on one of Hong Kong's most historic areas — Western District. This is where the docks were originally housed, an area traditionally dominated by Chiu Chows who came from further up the southeast coast of China and still carry on an active trade in commodities such as dried fish and ship-chandlers' supplies with their numerous cousins in Thailand. Further up the slopes one comes to the so-called Mid-Levels, a residential area dating back many years and which once boasted banyan trees and graceful Portuguese-style mansions. Many of these have now fallen into ruin or disrepair, but one of the loveliest sites is still visible from the Peak, the beautiful emerald garden in which stand the Synagogue and Jewish Recreation Club.

For those whose vantage points are limited to terra firma, it is, of course, from the Peak that one enjoys the most breathtaking panorama of Hong Kong. Reached by road or the Peak Tram — funicular railway — it is from here that the harbour stretches out beneath one in a bristling carpet of light blue sea, unwieldy super-tankers and gleaming cruise ships. Scurrying back and forth between them are the jetfoils and hydrofoils plying their trade between tiny, Portuguese-administered Macau with its successful tourism and alluring gambling industries.

The Peak has long been the traditional domain of business tycoons and British Government officials who tolerate the constant mist and fog largely for the prestige of actually living there. But gone is the excuse of the heat of the lower levels now that most people can afford a cooling system. Indeed, at his retirement after long service in Hong Kong a prominent British banker was asked what had made the most difference during his time here; the reply was unhesitating: "Air-conditioning".

Many from overseas who settle in Hong Kong tend to favour the luxury apartments along the island's south coast and this is now linked to Causeway Bay and the rest of the island's north shore by an impressive and time-saving road tunnel. There is also the heavily used road tunnel under the harbour and this is soon to be joined by the Eastern Harbour Crossing which will include both road and rail links and go some way to relieving the bottle necks and traffic jams during the more congested hours of travel.

The underwater tunnels are engineering miracles, consisting of long, concrete caissons sealed together in an open trench excavated on the seabed. The cross harbour tunnel in particular has materially altered the traffic patterns of Hong Kong, as previously vehicles could only cross the harbour on cumbersome ferries (now being used as temporary accommodation for refugees from Vietnam).

As the pictures in this remarkable book so clearly show, it is necessary to keep coming up with one expedient after another simply to keep the traffic flowing — and this is despite the Government's policy of extravagant registration taxes on motor vehicles and strict and demanding tests for learner drivers. Soon it will be a case of practically the whole island and much of the New Territories being ringed by super-highways from which will spread feeder roads into the urban areas. One of the most adventurous plans to ease the general circulation of traffic movement around Central District must be the scheme of an immense escalator snaking up into the Mid-Levels and intended to tap some of the demand on passenger and mini-buses as well as taxis and, of course, private cars themselves. The next collection of photographs could well show heavy vehicles banned completely from Central, thanks to fast and elevated detours. The same could go for the magnificent shopping malls of which new ones are planned for areas outside Central in yet another bid to cut down on crowding.

None of this, of course, will add to Hong Kong's beauty but the necessity to keep traffic moving takes precedence over scenic vistas or historical quaintness. Nevertheless, government landscape engineers do try to soften the harsher outlines of new roads or apartment blocks either by judicious planning of open spaces or the copious planting of flowering trees and shrubs. As for that other great artery of Hong Kong's transport lanes, Kai Tak airport, it has achieved the well-nigh impossible of establishing itself as the aviation hub of East Asia — with still only one runway! Something will eventually have to be done about building a new airport, and this will most likely be on one of the islands with some huge motor road linking it to Kowloon via yet another engineering miracle in the form of a long bridge.

With its nearly four million visitors a year, Hong Kong has to maintain its reputation as a major tourist attraction, and it is an added bonus that direct flights to Peking, Shanghai, Xi'an and other major Chinese cities now enable people to use Hong Kong as a jumping off point for tours of the People's Republic of China.

One needs only turn to the relevant photographs in this book to understand why people also come to Hong Kong to see its wild life. This ranges from the small but attractive aviary in the gardens just above Government House to the bird sanctuary at Mai Po Marshes in the New Territories and onto the most impressive of all, Ocean Park, the largest of its kind outside San Diego's Sea World. Here, in a gigantic plot just outside Aberdeen, one can see performing seals and porpoises, aquaria and a miniature zoo. The whole thing is linked to an equally popular aquatic funfair, Water World.

It is not surprising that the pressures of daily life in a city such as Hong Kong take their toll when it comes to an active cultural life; after all, it is demanding enough just to earn a living and find time to care for one's children. Nevertheless, the territory has an active and flourishing Art Centre backed up by a new Academy of Performing Arts, and various theatres and museums including the prominent dome-shaped Space Museum opposite the Peninsula Hotel in Kowloon.

If anything, the most popular pastime of the local Chinese is that of eating out and this, of course, means Chinese food of which Hong Kong offers a greater variety and of a higher standard than anywhere else in the world. Turning to those from overseas, what was once the traditional entertainment of visiting seamen or servicemen or, indeed, the more boisterous of the male 'expat' community has at last suffered a sea change and many of the once notorious Wanchai "girlie bars" have been flattened to make way for smart new office blocks or restaurants. Those that still ply this trade are mostly topless bars now and generally regarded as ruthless tourist traps, not to be ventured into by anyone lacking a firm grip on his wallet.

If at first glance these human aspects of Hong Kong seem difficult to discern from the aerial view, they are nevertheless very much in evidence in one larger sense and it is this: the story of Hong Kong is one about people whose extraordinary mastery of seemingly impossible problems has made them examples to an admiring world. Not least of their achievements has been to live together in such crowding and proximity and to bring to their daily lives and work both the discipline and the determination to carve a decent living environment out of an uncompromising terrain. It is a fascinating story and nowhere is that triumph more clearly seen than in the pages of this book.

Right
Victoria Harbour it was the harbour which first
attracted the British to Hong Kong. While the Kowloon
peninsula and Causeway Bay are at the left side, one can see the
island Eastern Corridor edging along the north side of the island
past North Point and Quarry Bay in the centre. On the other
side beyond Kai Tai airport is Kwun Tong, home to factories and
inexpensive housing estates.

THE ISLAND

Left
Victoria Harbour This *Aerospatiale SA 315B Lama* is a workhorse, a sort of aerial crane that also is ideal for high altitude mountain operations. If you want one of your own, Samaero of Singapore will gladly provide it for just over half a million US dollars!

Preceding page
Western Hong Kong Island Hong Kong Island is famous for having "every square inch of usable land built up" This crowding is nowhere more apparent than along the Central waterfront, though the contrast between the foreshore and the slopes of Victoria Peak above is striking. It is very hard to imagine what Hong Kong Island was like in 1841 when Captain Charles Elliot of the Royal Navy claimed possession by landing at Possession Point, a long since vanished promontory located somewhere behind the black and red towers of Shun Tak Centre which now grace the Western waterfront.

Right
Central at Christmas While it is deemed unsuitable that the British Forces headquarters, in the foreground, be lit up like a Christmas tree, the bronze Far East Finance Centre, the Bank of America Tower and the Hilton, centre left, show no such reticence. The arterial roads in the centre are Cotton Tree Drive, on the left, and Garden Road, with the new Peak Tram Terminus at the top where the roads appear to converge. The colonial building adjacent is the Helena May Club, with Government House lit up to the right.

Victoria Peak Spread behind the Peak itself are Kowloon's Ocean Terminal and Harbour City to the left and Central through to North Point and beyond on the right.

Bottom
The Peak Sprawling colonial-style residences in spacious grounds are still very much in evidence in the Peak area, remnants of an era when the wealthy few settled here to escape the oppressive heat, and create for themselves a little bit of England. But times have changed, as evidenced by the cityscape in the background, from Wanchai's circular Hopewell Centre, beyond the hill, to the white dome of the Space Museum and the glittering facade of the prestigious Regent hotel in Tsim Sha Tsui.

Right
The Peak Tower This is the terminus for the Peak Tram, the 99-year-old funicular railway which was once the only means available to reach the Peak. The red roof in the foreground belongs to The Peak Cafe, a quaint establishment serving snacks and teas in a garden setting. Highlights of the cityscape beyond include the HongkongBank, centre right, and Government House nestled in its lee. Across the harbour are Ocean Terminal, centre, Harbour City and Yau Ma Tei typhoon shelter to the left.

Above
The Peak Low-rise townhouse developments have become part of the luxury living scene on the Peak, onetime exclusive residential retreat for Hong Kong's wealthy *taipans*.

Above
Peak Tower The restaurant above the Peak Tram terminus, on the left, boasts extraordinary views of Hong Kong and Kowloon, while the colonial residential block, foreground, faces the island's south side.

Left
Central District Navy patrol boats ride at anchor opposite the black towers of Admiralty, with the United Centre behind and Far East Finance Centre to their right. Beyond, the striking twin-tower lines of the Bond Centre add more space-age style to a modern cityscape already greatly enhanced by the massive headquarters of the HongkongBank to the right, at No. 1, Queen's Road, Central.

Right
North Point and Quarry Bay Looking east from above the Braemar Hill residential complex at lower right, the new development emerging along the routes of the Island Eastern Corridor (the roadway at left) and the Island line of the Mass Transit Railway can be clearly seen. The rows of towers creeping up the valley at mid-right are the newly completed Kornhill Gardens, just to the south of Tai Koo Shing. which is a whole mini-city by itself. Soon, automobiles will be able to enter the second tunnel under the harbour from near here and travel directly to the eastern New Territories.

Left
Central District A unique bird's eye view of Hong Kong, the mass of green in the foreground includes the manicured confines of Government House, one of the territory's few remaining colonial buildings. The onetime panoramic harbour views enjoyed by its residents have long since been replaced by the vast high-rise developments of Central, traditionally Hong Kong's commercial hub. Latest in evidence is the futuristic headquarters of the Hongkong Bank, centre.

Left
Hongkong Bank Headquarters A striking contrast with its more sedate neighbours, the bank's avant garde design includes an atrium which rises 52 metres through 11 levels of the building from the public plaza.

Above
Hongkong Bank Headquarters Construction of the new building, third in a landmark series of Hongkong Bank headquarters, began on the 1 Queen's Road, Central, site in November 1981 and was completed in November, 1985. Designed by architect Norman Foster and built at a cost in the region of HK$5.3 billion, the building rises 52 levels, four of which are underground, and incorporates 28 lifts and 62 escalators, including the longest freely supported escalator in the world, which rises 25 metres from the public plaza to the banking hall.

▌Above
Wanchai Behind the Royal Navy yards, May House, the square white building housing Hong Kong's police headquarters, is dwarfed by the circular Hopewell Centre, Hong Kong's tallest building.

▌Upper right
Wanchai The Hong Kong Convention and Exhibition Centre, under construction in the foreground, will soon house two hotels and superb facilities. Government offices are based in the tower block at right.

▌Lower right
Wanchai A Royal Navy patrol boat, specially designed for local waters, is moored in the foreground, with the China Fleet Club, redeveloped by Hong Kong Land in 1985, far left.

▌Left
Central District In the heart of this classic Central view, the top of the Hilton Hotel and, to its right, the space-age tower of the Hongkong & Shanghai Bank are just visible, behind the Furama Hotel. At right is the Mandarin Hotel. Massive land reclamation projects have enabled Central to continue its burgeoning growth, making room for recent developments like the glimmering bronze Far East Finance Centre. The Prince of Wales Building, headquarters for the British forces, stands in the foreground, with an Australian navy ship at berth.

Happy Valley Racecourse Horse racing, along with the "Mark Six" lottery, being the only legalized forms of gambling in Hong Kong, it comes as no surprise that the Happy Valley track attracts capacity crowds during racing season, from mid-September to May. Chinese love a good gamble, so much so that total betting in a nine-month season can exceed HK$16 billion. Racing here, and at the Shatin track, is controlled by the Royal Hong Kong Jockey Club, a charitable organization which contributes millions annually to local charities and community activities.

Wong Nai Chung Gap Outdoor sports are popular in Hong Kong and clubs, like the Hong Kong Cricket Club, in the foreground, have expansive grounds which include pools, tennis courts and bowling greens among their facilities. Next door are the Wong Nai Chung Gap public courts. From this vantage point it is also possible to see the smoke stacks of Hong Kong's two major power stations, in Aberdeen and farther out on Lamma Island. Deep Water Bay Road winds down around the residential district of Shouson Hill and on to Aberdeen.

Left
Causeway Bay Boats rest at anchor at the Royal Hong Kong Yacht Club whose clubhouse, the circular building on the point, was once surrounded by water. The area is Kellett Island now in name only, the result of reclamation work. To the left of the club is the slanting entrance to the Cross Harbour Tunnel and, next to that, the new police recreation club. The Hong Kong-Macau Ferry Terminal, with its distinctive horizontal red stripes, can be seen at the opposite end of the waterfront.

Above
Causeway Bay Sampans cluster next to the police recreation club, at this stage still under construction. Opposite is the rounded facade of the Excelsior Hotel and its towering neighbour, the World Trade Centre. Green patches of the Happy Valley racecourse can be glimpsed beyond and, on the hilly horizon to the left, Wong Nai Chung Gap.

Following page
Causeway Bay Dusk settles on Causeway Bay, almost time for the world's largest neon, the Citizen sign atop Elizabeth House, to light up the night. In the foreground the new police recreation club perches beside the entrance to the Cross Harbour Tunnel, and behind that stands the heart of Causeway Bay with its innumerable shops, department stores and restaurants. The flyover through the buildings to the right leads to Happy Valley, its racecourse just visible, while the Noonday Gun, immortalized by Noel Coward, stands in the enclosure opposite the Excelsior.

Preceding page
Island Eastern Corridor With less than
1,500 kilometres of roads and some 270,000
vehicles using them, traffic density is a perennial
problem in Hong Kong. Congestion has been
dramatically reduced by the Eastern Island
Corridor from Causeway Bay to Shau Kei Wan,
seen here sweeping past the Causeway Bay
typhoon shelter and Victoria Park, North Point and
Tai Koo Shing. The shining black building, centre, is
the new headquarters for Citibank. Note the
aircraft which has just taken off from the runway
across the harbour at Kai Tak.

Above
Tai Koo Shing Squatter huts perch
precariously on the hills overlooking the high-
density residential area of Tai Koo Shing, a
51-tower property development by John Swire
and Sons Limited, housing upwards of 50,000
people in the eastern district of Hong Kong Island.
Across the water, Hong Kong's famous airport
runway at Kai Tak stretches out into the harbour.

Above
Southside of Hong Kong Island The fisheye lens captures a sweeping view of the south side of the island. Starting from upper left and continuing counter-clockwise, you can see Bluff's Head at the very tip of Stanley Peninsula, the residences of Repulse Bay opposite Middle Island, the Royal Hong Kong Golf Club course on Deepwater Bay, the tollbooths at the entry to the Aberdeen Tunnel, Aberdeen Harbour, and the smokestacks of the power station on Lamma Island at upper right.

Left
Chung Hom Kok Luxury low-rise residences perch on the headland at Chung Hom Kok, along with a neighbouring squatters' shanty-town. The headland features, at its base, a pleasant bathing beach rarely as crowded as its near neighbours, Repulse Bay and Stanley, due to the area's relative inaccessbility and the steep descent to the shore. Low-rise enclaves such as this have become increasingly popular throughout the territory in recent years, among both expatriates and the swelling ranks of young middle class Chinese.

Right
Tai Tam Just past Stanley, if you travel east on the Tai Tam Road, are The Manhattan luxury apartments, all facing the sea. In typical Hong Kong fashion, this tower was developed by a clothing manufacturer, Manhattan Garments Limited. Residents enjoy a spectacular view across Tai Tam Bay towards D'Aguilar Point. The American Club at Tai Tam is on the shore.

Left
Stanley Headland The largest settlement on Hong Kong Island before the British arrived in 1841, Stanley today is a peaceful residential district straddling the southernmost peninsula of Hong Kong. Among its attractions are good beaches — Stanley Beach on the right and Turtle Cove on the left — and a popular shopping village. Stanley Prison is the white rectangular complex on the left, while the green oval to its right belongs to St. Stephens College. Telecommunications discs and military installations occupy the headland beyond.

Above
Container Ship Looking as much like a freight train as a ship, the *Louis Maersk* cuts through the South China Sea on its way from the Kwai Chung terminals to overseas ports. With the second busiest port in the world after Rotterdam, Hong Kong's trade continues to grow rapidly. In the first six months of 1987, the volume increased 30 percent over the same period in the previous year.

Above

Repulse Bay Bathers crowd the shore every summer
at Repulse Bay, Hong Kong Island's most accessible and
popular beach. The famous old Repulse Bay Hotel once
occupied the gap in the landscape to the left and, since this
picture was taken, the hotel's ever-popular Verandah
Restaurant has been reconstructed, down to the finest detail,
on the site.

Right
Repulse Bay This headland juts out between Repulse Bay, off the picture to the right, and Deep Water Bay on the left. Some of Hong Kong's wealthiest families live in the exclusive residences occupying the foreshore. Behind them Repulse Bay Road snakes up towards Wong Nai Chung Gap, through which the high-rise developments of Causeway Bay and North Point are plainly visible. The triangle of green stretching up the hill behind Deep Water Bay is the nine-hole golf course of the prestigious Royal Hong Kong Golf Club.

Above
Tai Tam The new American Club facility at Tai Tam is informally known as the "Country Club" to distinguish it from the "Town Club" located in Central District. The view is said to be as spectacular as any in the Mediterranean, while the building was designed to make a Southern Californian feel right at home.

Right
Repulse Bay Pleasure craft ride at anchor beyond the safety netting which encircles popular Repulse Bay Beach on the south side of Hong Kong Island. Rising in the background is Violet Hill, a regular haunt for hikers, with Deepwater Bay beyond the headland to the left. It was only some 55 years ago that the first road, passing through Wong Nei Chong Gap, centre back, made ready access to this area a reality, and the luxury residential building boom was quick to follow.

Top right
Ocean Park The longest outdoor escalator in the world snakes up to the headland restaurants and entertainments which include Wave Cove on the left and Ocean Theatre, centre.

Bottom right
Ocean Park The largest entertainment complex in Southeast Asia, Ocean Park also boasts one of the longest and fastest roller-coaster rides in the world.

Left
Water World Currently funded by the Royal Hong Kong Jockey Club, Ocean Park is an 87-hectare fun park and oceanarium on the south side of Hong Kong Island. Some 1.5 million visitors passed through its doors in 1986, attracted by the thrill rides, Ocean Theatre, the children's zoo, *Cine 2000* and, not least, Water World. The first water play park of its kind in Asia, Water World is in the lowland area and attracts up to 6,000 visitors a day in the summer months.

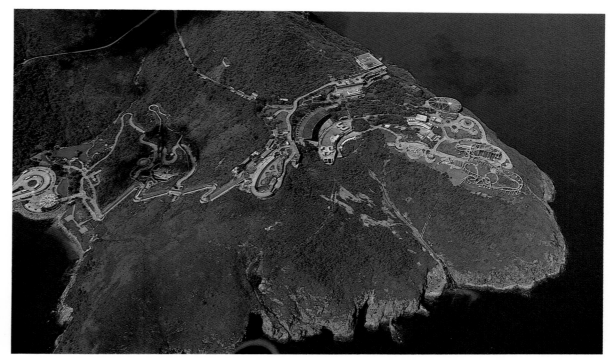

Above
Water World Children armed with bright red floating rings line up for a slipping sliding ride at Water World, part of the huge Ocean Park entertainment complex.

Above
Wah Fu Estate The first major public housing estate to be built on Hong Kong Island, Wah Fu will see further expansion when reclamation work in Kellett Bay is completed.

Right
Aberdeen Floating Restaurants In the densely packed harbour at Aberdeen, it is impossible to avoid the three huge floating restaurants. Flanked by the boat people on one side, and the James Bond-style luxury cruisers moored at the Aberdeen Marina Club on the other, these restaurants specialize in local seafood with Jumbo, in the centre, able to feed up to 5,000 people at a sitting. It is said Hong Kong got its name, "Fragrant Harbour", from an incense factory here which regularly filled the harbour with the smell of burning joss sticks.

Left
Aberdeen Marina Club A recent addition to the ranks of exclusive Hong Kong clubs, the Marina with its roof-top swimming pool and tennis courts offers its members gracious dining and diverse recreational facilities. The Jumbo floating restaurant occupies the foreground and a public swimming pool complex, built with funds made available by shipping magnate, Sir Y.K. Pao, is at back.

Above
Queen Elizabeth II Cunard's famous *QE II* passes by on its way to berth at Ocean Terminal. Approximately four percent of Hong Kong's nearly four million tourists arrive by ship, surely the most elegant way to travel to the territory. The *QE II* herself visits Hong Kong only occasionally during her world cruises, but each time she brings over a thousand passengers for a few days of sightseeing and shopping.

Left
Chi Fu Fa Yuen Originally developed by Hong Kong Land, the residential estate of Chi Fu stands above Pokfulam Road midway between Pokfulam and Aberdeen, on what was once lush farmland owned by the Dairy Farm Company. This self-contained estate includes a range of sporting facilities, from the circular roller-skating rink, centre, to an indoor swimming pool and a bowling alley, together with a traditional-style market and a modern shopping centre. Matilda Hospital, at top right, and luxury Peak residential blocks occupy the lofty background heights.

Left
Green Island Across the Sulphur Channel from Kennedy Tower on the western tip of Hong Kong Island, appropriately named Green Island houses a Signal Station operated by the Marine Department. And while isolated, life for the staff looks as though it may have its compensating factors, like the occasional swim. Better in a pool than the harbour waters too, if that seasonal tide of debris is anything to go by.

Right
Pok Fu Lam Trade with the mainland represents a major economic force in the local economy, and China is the second largest importer of goods produced in Hong Kong, as well as being its largest supplier of imported foodstuffs and other items. Much of China's trade with the rest of the world is conducted through Hong Kong through the numerous import-export companies in the territory. This ship of the People's Republic is heading south past Pok Fu Lam, below Victoria Peak at left and Mount Kellet.

■ Above
Pokfulam Victoria Peak towers above this popular residential district, with Queen Mary Hospital standing at the heart of its base. On the waterfront, to the right, are the tall circular Hong Kong University staff quarters while in the centre, scenic villas shimmer in the sun. The large grey section up to the left is the Mount Davis cemetery.

Right
Baguio Villas Hong Kong's first major high-density luxury residential development, with in excess of 1,500 flats, Baguio Villas were some four years in the making and completed in 1980. Although most apartments are owned by private individuals, New World Development, who developed this site along with Hong Kong landmarks like the New World Hotel and shopping complex in Tsim Sha Tsui, retained two towers for rental purposes. Flats range in size from a modest 1,020 square feet to a very spacious 2,800 square feet.

Above
Shun Tak Centre The twin towers of the Shun Tak Centre in Western District house numerous shops and offices as well as the Hotel Victoria and the Hong Kong-Macau Ferry Terminal.

Right
Western District
Dominating the Western waterfront is the new Shun Tak Centre and Hong Kong-Macau Ferry Terminal. Some 9.5 million passengers journey the 64 kilometres between Portuguese Macau, on the Pearl River estuary, and Hong Kong each year. Moving along the waterfront past Central and Wanchai, the white club-house of the Royal Hong Kong Yacht Club sits in front of the Causeway Bay typhoon shelter. And across the harbour in Tsim Sha Tsui, the Regent and the New World Hotel and shopping complex occupy the point.

Right
Kowloon Looking roughly northeast from over Central District, Kowloon lies under a scattering of clouds. Kowloon means 'Nine Dragons', and until 1860 remained a part of the Chinese Empire. Officially, Kowloon proper only extends as far as Boundary Street, extending from the waterfront at the lower left edge of the photo all the way to the northwest corner of the airport. Beyond is the New Territories, but crossing Boundary Street you would never be able to tell, as Hong Kong's urbanisation continues apace. To the right can be seen North Point.

KOWLOON

Left
Tsim Sha Tsui The people of Hong Kong love a good celebration and top of the long list are Christmas and Chinese New Year. Here Tsim Sha Tsui East's hotels and shopping centres are seen dressed for the occasion, from the Regent and New World jutting into the harbour on the point, to the Holiday Inn Harbour View with its roof-top swimming pool at the opposite end of the waterfront row. The line of lights running up the heart of the peninsula is Chatham Road.

Preceding page
Tsim Sha Tsui Car ferries ply their cross-harbour routes with the grand sweep of Tsim Sha Tsui's western waterfront in the background. Developed by the Hongkong & Kowloon Wharf & Godown Company, this complex includes, from the right, Star House, Ocean Centre, Ocean Terminal, Harbour Centre and three international hotels, making it the largest interconnected shopping complex in Southeast Asia. Kowloon Peak rises 602 metres to the left and the airport runway at Kai Tak juts into the harbour behind the point.

Above
Star Ferry Terminal Still the best value in town, the ten distinctive green and white ferries of the Star Ferry service have been carrying passengers from Central District on Hong Kong Island to Tsim Sha Tsui since 1898. The eight-minute journey, costing just HK70 cents first class and HK50 cents for a second class seat on the lower deck, is an unbeatable opportunity to see Hong Kong at its best, from the water. Appropriately, all the boats are named after stars, *Celestial Star* and *Twinkling Star* to name a few.

Left
Mongkok and Ho Man Tin Mongkok is believed to be the most densely populated area in the world, with more than 150,000 people for each square kilometre. Yet just to the east (at top) of the Kowloon-Canton Railroad tracks running from left to right at centre is the much more gracious living of Ho Man Tin. The Yaumatei typhoon shelter is at bottom, while the ferry pier to China at Tai Kok Tsui is just to the north of it.

Right
Cross-Harbour Tunnel Peak-hour traffic can be daunting for commuters between Hong Kong Island and Kowloon, with the only current alternatives being a slow crawl through the Cross-Harbour Tunnel and an equally sedate, if more scenic, crossing on a car ferry. But plans are underway to relieve the considerable congestion on the world's busiest four-lane facility, with the construction of the Eastern Harbour Crossing which will include both road and rail links.

Above
Container Ship Small but powerful, tugboats
maneuver the ungainly bulk of yet another ship to its berth.

Right
Douglas DC-3 This famous aeroplane is fondly called
'Betsy' by Cathay Pacific. In 1946 Betsy, a former C-47 military transport, became the first aircraft of the newly formed
company, flying to Manila, Bangkok, Singapore and Sydney.
After a thirty-year absence, the plane was returned to Hong
Kong in 1983 from its previous home in Australia, repainted in
its original Cathay livery and is now kept at the international
airport.

Left
Tsim Sha Tsui Nathan Road, Tsim Sha Tsui's main thoroughfare, stretches up the peninsula from opposite the domed Space Museum with, on the lefthand corner, the famous Peninsula Hotel and, on the right, the Sheraton. Moving along Nathan Road on the left, there are the black-fronted Kowloon Hotel and the Hyatt in the next block. The Holiday Inn Golden Mile is opposite, with its roof-top swimming pool and its none-too-salubrious next-door neighbour, Chungking House, a rabbit warren of shops, Indian cafes and guesthouses.

Right
Regent and New World Hotels One of a prestigious international chain, the Hong Kong Regent, forefront, enjoys an enviable waterfront location alongside the New World shopping, apartment and hotel complex. In the background red-roofed buses line up at the traffic lights on Chatham Road with Signal Hill Garden on the left and the start of Tsim Sha Tsui East to the right.

Left
Tsim Sha Tsui East A recently developed area even by Hong Kong standards, Tsim Sha Tsui East has managed to avoid the dense high-rise clutter so typical of Kowloon. World-class hotels, like the Regent and New World, far left, and the Shangri-La, the Regal Meridien and the Holiday Inn Harbour View, on the front roads, occupy much of the area, along with ultra-modern shopping complexes. Beyond Chatham Road which begins opposite the New World Hotel, is Tsim Sha Tsui proper, including the white dome of the Space Museum.

Above
Tsim Sha Tsui East Testimony to the dynamism of Hong Kong, this glittering stretch was a barren wasteland ten years ago. Included here are the Empire Centre, front right, and behind it the Regal Meridien, with the Tsim Sha Tsui Centre, the Shangri-La and Wing On Plaza stretching to Chatham Road where double-decker buses are stopped at traffic lights opposite the New World Hotel. That Hong Kong is the world's second busiest port in terms of container throughput is evidenced by the number of ships at anchor on the horizon.

Following page
Kowloon Peninsula An extraordinary 2.5 million of Hong Kong's population, now in excess of 5.6 million, live on the Kowloon Peninsula, making it one of the most densely populated pieces of land on earth. In the northwest, a cross-harbour car ferry has just left the Yau Ma Tei typhoon shelter on route to Central, while an aircraft is taxiing down the runway which juts into the harbour at Kai Tak, to the northeast. The clocktower, foreground, is all that remains of the old Kowloon-Canton Railway Terminus.

Upper Tsim Sha Tsui Looking from above the Kowloon-Canton Railway Station at Hung Hom, one sees first the entrance to the Cross Harbour Tunnel, the world's busiest four-lane facility, used by 110,500 vehicles per day in 1986. The cluster of brown buildings beyond make up the Hong Kong Polytechnic, while behind them lies the white and green sprawl of the Gun Club Hill Barracks and Kowloon's Bowling Green Club. Again in the foreground, the sleek grey building with red doors is the Tsim Tum Fire Station and Fire Services Headquarters.

Hong Kong Coliseum The largest indoor stadium in Hong Kong, the Coliseum, foreground, seats 12,500 for a wide range of sporting spectaculars, concerts and entertainment events, including performances by celebrities like Frank Sinatra and world-ranking athletes. The arena can also be converted into an ice rink for ice-skating shows and recreational purposes. The entrance to the Cross Harbour Tunnel lies to the left of the Coliseum and, beyond the major overpass which is Cheong Wan Road, are the brown cluster of the Hong Kong Polytechnic buildings.

| Above

Hung Hom On the waterfront behind the public swimming pool complex, the old Whampoa dockyard has been levelled to make way for Whampoa Gardens, a huge residential complex. Most of this bay will soon be reclaimed to house a massive freightyard for the Kowloon-Canton Railway and, on a 14-hectare podium above it, a residential estate.

| Right

Hong Kong International Airport Traffic through the airport at Kai Tak has seen rapid continuous growth in recent years, with some 10.6 million passengers and 536,000 tonnes of cargo passing through in 1986. In the same year, an 8.5 percent increase in aircraft movements brought the total to 64,700. Work to extend the airport passenger terminal building will be completed shortly, almost doubling the capacity to 18 million passengers. Beyond the airport are the industrial and residential areas of Ngau Tau Kok and Kwun Tong.

Above
Airliners at Kai Tak Surprisingly small to those who have not seen it before and an unusual visitor to Hong Kong, is the Concorde. This Air France plane was on a special charter when it was photographed. Normally the supersonic jet, which carries only a hundred passengers, travels the New York to Paris route in an amazingly short three and a half hours.

Right
Hong Kong International Airport Though this is the official name of Hong Kong's only airport, to residents it is familiarly known as 'Kai Tak'. Boundary Street, which technically divides Kowloon from the New Territories, angles off to the upper right, while the infamous Kai Tak nullah, responsible for the none-too-pleasant aroma greeting arriving passengers, can be seen flowing from right to left.

Right
New Territories The diversity of life and style in Hong Kong is perhaps most vivid in the New Territories, where the towers of new towns like Tai Po suddenly soar out of a landscape of traditional gardens and fields; and where people seek out havens in their own kinds of communities, whether in an isolated development of low-rise luxury homes on the northwest coast or a harbour full of sampans near Tuen Mun.

NEW TERRITORIES AND THE OUTLYING ISLANDS

▌Preceding page
Highways Key to the success of the burgeoning new towns, dotted throughout the New Territories, are the strategic road and rail networks linking the towns both with each other and the centralized business and commercial centres. The Kowloon-Canton Railway, seen here, also plays a vital role in transporting freight between Hong Kong and China. In 1986, some 3.28 million tonnes of freight and 2.21 million head of livestock entered the territory by rail, and 848,000 tonnes of goods were exported to China by the same route.

▌Above
Approaching Kwai Chung An American President Lines container ship is on its way to be loaded at the Kwai Chung terminals. If it is typical, it's likely to be back at sea a mere 13 hours after it arrives, the world's fastest turn-around time.

▌Right
Kwai Chung Container Port Huge the terminal already is, but expansion plans have been well underway since 1984, with a total of 55 hectares of seabed at Kwai Chung Creek being reclaimed. The additional space will enable three more berths to be added to the existing facilities which can simultaneously accommodate six 'third generation' container vessels.

Left

Tsing Yi Island Part of the Tsuen Wan New Town,
Tsing Yi has already seen rapid development as an industrial
site on the southern and western parts of the island. The
next phase, already well underway, is the construction of
large public housing estates over the next few years. Of
prime importance to these developments is transport and
the new Tsing Yi North Bridge, seen here and expected to
be completed in late 1989, will do much to relieve the severe
congestion on the single bridge currently connecting the
island with the mainland.

Right
Tsing Yi Island One of the relatively few heavy industrial sites in Hong Kong, Tsing Yi Island houses several large shipbuilding and repair yards which are generally recognized as among the best available in Asia. As well as ships and cruisers of all shapes and sizes, oil rigs are constructed and launched here, predominantly for use in the South China Sea. Seen here in the centre of the bay is an unusual floating dockyard, one innovative solution to insufficient space on land.

Above
Tsing Yi Island An ocean-going freighter is undergoing repair work on the massive floating drydock situated in the heavy industrial southwestern section of Tsing Yi Island.

Right
Tsing Yi Island Part of Tsuen Wan New Town, along with nearby Kwai Chung container terminal, Tsing Yi Island is connected with the mainland by bridge. The industrial section which covers the southern and western parts of the island enjoys an international reputation for its fast and efficient shipbuilding and repair services. As well oil rigs, like the one seen here, are regularly built and serviced at the shipyards. The lighters in the background are loading containers for removal to Kwai Chung.

▌Above

Tuen Mun In 1980, this point of reclaimed land was completely undeveloped. Today, a whole miniature city has risen here, just to the south of the centre of Tuen Mun New Town, with names such as Butterfly Estate, Melody Garden and the like. The southeastern tip of the peninsula points towards the Pearl Island luxury development which can just be seen jutting out into Castle Peak Bay. The ferry that travels from the pier on the right provides residents with an enjoyable direct commute to Central District.

Above
Above
Pearl Island Not all construction in the new towns has
been high-density high-rise, as witnessed by this attractive
townhouse development on Pearl Island near Tuen Mun
township, in the northwestern New Territories. In recent
years, small residential enclaves such as this have become
increasingly popular among Hong Kong's burgeoning young
middle class. Work has also begun on a marina in the area,
which will provide hotel and commercial facilities as well as
berths for 300 craft.

Left

Tuen Mun The third new town to be launched, after Tsuen Wan and Shatin, Tuen Mun's population has already reached some 280,000 and is expected to pass the 500,000 mark by the mid-1990s. Castle Peak Bay, in the foreground, has been and will continue to be the site of major reclamation work and it is here that the high-density urban core is situated. The town is also spreading rapidly up the valley between Castle Peak, on the left, and the Tai Lam hills.

Above

Tsuen Wan One of the first generation of new towns, Tsuen Wan was developed as an industrial satellite of urban Kowloon in the post-war years. The thriving township, seen here, currently houses some 700,000 people. To cope with an expected increase in population of 100,000 by the early 1990s, reclamation work already underway in Tsuen Wan Bay will create land for a modern residential and commercial development. This, it is hoped, should do much to relieve the pressures on the older, congested town centre.

Above
Tsuen Wan On the hills above Tsuen Wan,
Wonderland Villas, centre, command a stunning view of the
entire Kowloon Peninsula, Kowloon Reservoir and Hong
Kong Island. In the hazy distance to the left, the airport
runway juts into the harbour at Kai Tak. The finger of land at
top right is Stonecutters Island, still under military use.

Above
Tai Po Historically a bustling little market town for its rural hinterland, Tai Po New Town today includes a 69-hectare industrial estate and houses a population of some 140,000. This figure is expected to rise to 300,000 by the mid-1990s and six new public housing estates to accommodate the growth are in the pipeline. The township centres on the northwestern tip of Tolo Harbour.

Following page
Fish Ponds Ponds such as these near Yuen Long New Town take up approximately two percent of Hong Kong's land area and furnish an annual average of some 5,700 tonnes of freshwater fish. Farming methods are traditional, with a variety of carp species being the main product. Many farmers also breed ducks as a lucrative sideline.

Above
Sampans The boat people, or *Tanka*, decorate their
boats with gaily-coloured flags of good fortune for festivals
and weddings. Of particular importance to the boat people is
the festival of Tin Hau, the goddess who began life as the
daughter of a fisherman and saved a fleet from a violent typhoon. Some of the *Tanka* are quite rich but prefer to keep
their wealth in gold bullion and jewellery on their boats, which
leaves them vulnerable to loss from fire.

Right
Lighters While containerization has changed the face of
cargo handling operations in Hong Kong, more traditional
methods remain very much in evidence. Lighters — there are
about 2,000 of these work horses of cargo handling afloat —
cluster here around a recently arrived vessel, one of the some
15,000 ocean-going cargo ships that call in to Hong Kong each
year. Lighters, like fishing junks, often double as floating homes
for the families who operate them.

Left
Fairview Park Surrounded by the protected Mai Po Marshes, on the northwest coast of the New Territories, this luxury residential development offers low-rise living and excellent facilities for those keen to escape the pressures of inner- city dwelling. The peak to the right is Kai Keung Leng, Fanling New Town rises in the background and Shenzhen lies to the left.

Right
Hong Lok Yuen Just off the main highway between the New Towns of Shatin and Fanling can be found this self-enclosed neighborhood of luxury homes. Skirting the community on the west is the railway to the People's Republic, just ten kilometres to the north.

Above
Cessna 182 One of the many aerial pleasures available in Hong Kong is skydiving, here performed over Sek Kong in the middle of the New Territories. (Photographed by Robbie Shaw)

Right
Mudry CAP 10B This acrobatic aeroplane is flying against the backdrop of terrain that surprisingly resembles the barren islands off the coast of Alaska in summer. In actuality, this is part of Plover Cove Country Park, with Mirs Bay in the background and mainland China beyond. (Photographed by Robbie Shaw)

Riverside Village While rural isolation has always held appeal in Western societies and not being able to see one's neighbour is considered an asset, many Asians prefer to cluster together for security and company. This riverside village in the northwestern New Territories, home to fish pond farmers in the main, is no exception. And makeshift though it may appear, the village manages to withstand floods and typhoons, and provide a comfortable home for its residents.

Fish Ponds Pale, elongated shadows stretch out from the line of trees in the foreground across these fish ponds near Yuen Long New Town. As with traditional Chinese pond fish farming, ponds like these contain several species of carp, and often ducks, enabling the greatest benefit to be reaped from the variety of food sources available.

Pak Nai Silt from the Pearl River estuary makes Deep Bay, pictured in the foreground, a rather shallow and unappealing sight for much of the year. But the fertile pocket it borders, up in the northwestern New Territories, is a picture-book example of traditional small plot farming with different fields devoted to rice, vegetables, fish and ducks. Oysters are also farmed along the foreshore of this area which borders Lau Fau Shan to the north and Yuen Long to the east.

Above
Tiger Moth Tigers were last sighted stalking the woods of the New Territories very early in this century. But this one stalked the skies as recently as two years ago. Brought here in 1976 by Captain Dave Baker and superbly restored to its original condition, this deHavilland *Tiger Moth* was built in 1941 and saw service as a training aircraft until 1946. Captain Baker kept it at Sek Kong in the New Territories before moving it to a new home in Australia.

Left
Shatin New Town One of the first generation of new towns and certainly the show piece development, Shatin has seen explosive growth in recent years, with the population expanding from 100,000 to 400,000 in 1986, and expected to reach 750,000 by the mid-1990s. Built along Shing Mun River, the territory's premier international rowing and dragon boat racing course, Shatin enjoys a prosperous atmosphere and excellent facilities, including Shatin racecourse, across the river, Jubilee Sports Centre, adjacent, the territory's hub for amateur sports, and the horizontal-H-shaped Riverside Plaza Hotel.

Above
Traffic Accident With approximately one automobile, bus or truck for every seventeen Hong Kong residents, accidents are bound to happen, and traffic jams are common on the oftentimes intricate road system.

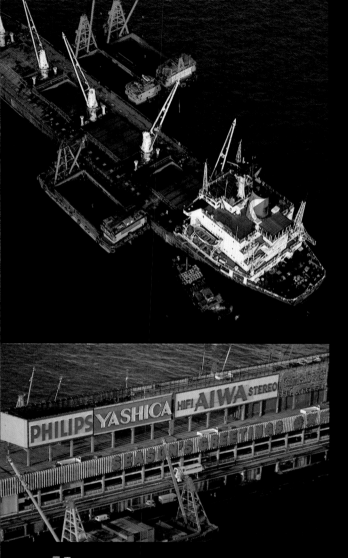

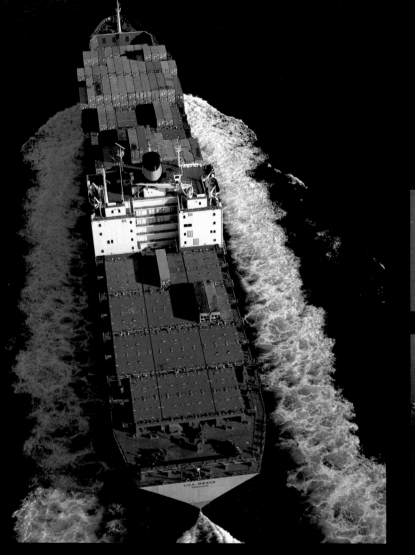

■ Top
Lighters Although container terminals have become the order of the day, some 2,000 lighters are still in use in the port moving cargo to and from ships' holds.

■ Bottom
Ocean Terminal Rearing up behind the neons that decorate the roof of Ocean Terminal are several booms of the ubiquitous lighters, busy shifting containers from storage and the deck area.

■ Above
Container Ship Some 14,050 ocean-going ships and a staggering 81,150 river-trade vessels called at Hong Kong in 1986, loading and discharging more than 62 million tonnes of cargo.

■ Top
Watertours It was the superb harbour which made Hong Kong and Watertours offer a variety of cruises which give passengers a comfortable glimpse at its beauty and multiple functions.

■ Middle
Fishing Boat Hong Kong's fishing fleet is the largest and certainly the most efficient on the South China Coast, with some 24,000 fishermen manning more than 4,700 vessels.

■ Bottom
U.S. Aircraft Carrier Hong Kong has long been a popular liberty port for the U.S. Seventh Fleet and off-duty sailors still flock to Wanchai in search of the fabled Suzie Wong.

Above
Sai Kung Northeast of the Kowloon Peninsula, sheltered little beaches like this one in Sai Kung Country Park offer a welcome respite from the densely packed urban areas. Country parks play an important recreational role in Hong Kong, and the more remote ones like this are popular venues for hiking, picnicking, camping, cycling and kite flying. In the region of 9.4 million visits were made to the country parks in 1986, a clear indication of the significant part they play in enhancing the leisure time activities of Hong Kong people.

Right
Peng Chau Island Farming and fishing have been the main stays of the community on Peng Chau for centuries and, while the tiny island is only an hour from Central District by ferry, it could well be a whole world away. Surrounded by the South China Sea, Peng Chau's nearest neighbours are Lantau Island on the right, Hei Ling Chau — a closed centre for some 2,000 Vietnamese refugees — beyond, and Cheung Chau just visible behind.

Above
Marina Cove Situated along the Ho Chung River (at bottom) which empties into the quiet bay known as Hebe Haven, Marina Cove offers a unique attraction: a boat club at your doorstep. Not all of the residents have boats, however, and not all members of the Club Marina Cove live in the project. This combination has proven to be equally popular with affluent expatriates and Chinese. After all, the ability to just take off on a boat and spend a leisurely day exploring the quiet bays and beautiful islands that remind many of Scotland is one of the greatest joys of Hong Kong living.

Right
Sai Kung Some 40 percent of Hong Kong's land area is covered by 21 country parks featuring spectacular hill and coastal scenery. This area, in the region of Junk Bay, is a popular hiking and camp site. Chai Wan, to the east on Hong Kong Island, rises in the middle background with, through the narrow Lei Yue Mun Channel to the right, parts of Shau Kei Wan and North Point just visible on the horizon.

Sok Kwu Wan Getting away from it all is no mean feat in Hong Kong, and pleasure boats play a central role in whisking parties intent on escape to tiny havens like Sok Kwu Wan on southern Lamma Island. Here they can feast on excellent seafood, much of it "cultivated" in the fish farms clustered in the foreground, in surroundings as unpretentious as they are colourful. Set on the eastern shore of Picnic Bay, Sok Kwu Wan is just a short cruise from Aberdeen on Hong Kong Island.

Junk Increasingly rare, wind-powered junks are a special treat when sighted; sometimes they appear from the Chinese mainland carrying a cargo of vegetables or pigs to help stock the many street markets in Hong Kong. Before motorisation, junk trawlers fished primarily during the winter months when the winds were stronger; today, fresh fish is available all year round.

Left
Clearwater Bay Golf Course After difficult beginnings which almost saw the club bankrupted, the Clearwater Bay Golf and Country Club has emerged as one of the most sought-after country club memberships in the territory. Set high on the peninsula with spectacular views of the rugged coast and mountainous hinterland, the challenging course offers an enjoyable game as well as a complete escape from the rigours of life in Hong Kong. Fish farmers ply their trade in the sheltered cove to the left.

Preceding page
Discovery Bay A recently developed residential area on Lantau Island, Discovery Bay's main attractions are space, low-rise living and superb recreational facilities. Only 25 minutes from Central by fast hover ferry, seen here departing from the wharf, Discovery Bay enjoys all the advantages of the leisurely outlying island life without the disadvantage of tedious commuting times. Sailing and windsurfing are popular pursuits here and community facilities in the development range from a pleasant golf course to tennis and squash courts and an Olympic-size swimming pool.

Right
Sharp Mountain In the northeastern New Territories, to the north of High Island Reservoir, rugged Sharp Mountain rises 468 metres above the tiny farming hamlet of Tai Long. Most of this secluded area is controlled by the Country Parks Authority and is quite inaccessible by road.

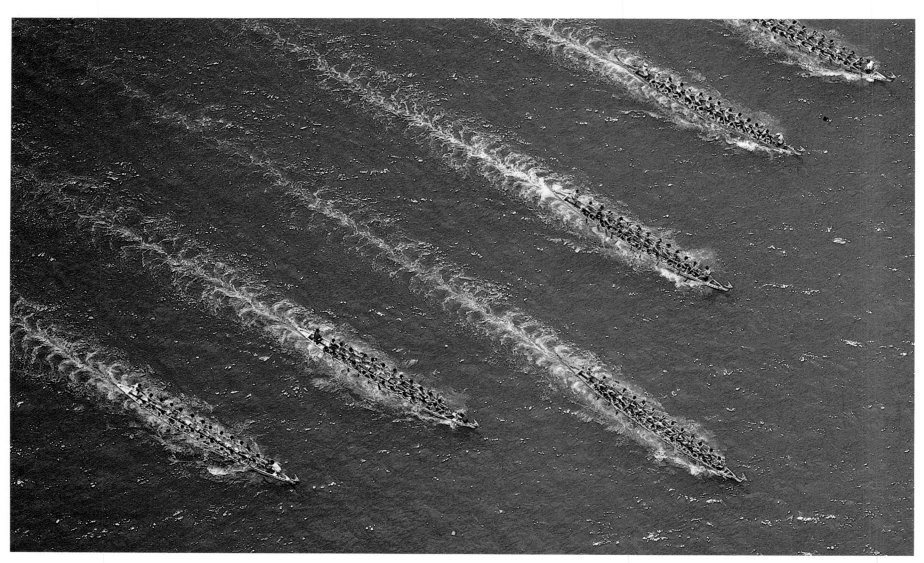

Above
Dragon Boat Races Local legend has it that these annual boat races commemorate the suicide by drowning of an ancient court scholar in protest against the official corruption of the times. Whatever the reason, the Dragon Boat Festival has become a celebration with enormous popular appeal, and rowing teams of ten to twenty practise months in advance for the big day.

Right
Sharp Mountain Those wishing to emulate these hardy souls standing victoriously on the summit of Sharp Mountain may find the long trek to the base of the peak adventure enough. No roads lead to this craggy spot, but the stunning views out across Long Harbour to the left, Tap Mun Chau and Port Island beyond the summit, and Mirs Bay beyond must make the journey worthwhile.

Above
Dragon Boat Mishap Dragon boat racing requires
greater skill and discipline than it might appear to an observer.
It is impossible to tell from the air, but it is a fair bet that a
non-Chinese team has come to grief here. Traditionally fishing
villages fielded the teams for the annual races, but today busi-
nesses and goverment departments also join in the fun.

Above
Shipwreck During typhoon season, usually between
July and October, Hong Kong is regularly lashed by tropical
cyclones, gale-force winds and tornadoes. But with the
sophisticated tracking and warning systems now in use, the
incidence of damage and loss of life has declined. Most
severely affected generally are the ships that didn't quite
make it to port.

USS Carl Vinson One of the Nimitz-class nuclear-powered carriers, the *USS Carl Vinson* was commissioned in 1975, but it took seven years for this state-of-the-art ship to be built. Despite its small appearance, the *Vinson* can hold up to 90 aircraft. Hong Kong has long been a favourite port of call for sailors of many nations. Each year, over 35,000 naval personnel visit Hong Kong, making a sizeable contribution to the territory's tourist revenue.

Above
USS Midway This venerable American ship is conventionally powered and based in Japan. Though many American naval vessels stop in Hong Kong, no manoeuvers are conducted in the vicinity: the *Midway* primarily operates in the western Pacific as part of the Seventh Fleet.

▌Top
Westland Scout AH1 Three Army Air Corps 'copters of the 660 Squadron fly just west of Castle Peak, near Tuen Mun. (Photographed by Robbie Shaw)

▌Bottom
Westland Wessex MC2 A helicopter of the 28th Squadron of the Royal Air Force hovers above Lion Rock. (Photographed by Robbie Shaw)

Above
Cheung Chau Fishing is the mainstay of many residents of Cheung Chau, literally "Long Island", a small, densely populated outlying island one hour from Central District by ferry. Its sheltered harbour, protected by a typhoon breakwater, is crowded with big traditional fishing junks, many of them produced by local master boatbuilders who scorn the use of blueprints and work purely from memory. Cars are entirely banned on Cheung Chau, a welcome change and a very necessary one given the narrowness and clutter of the village's winding alleys.

Gardens near Sek Kong Market gardening is still done the time-honoured Chinese way in the New Territories, with the relatively small patches of fertile land intensively cultivated. Farmers here are also masters of crop rotation and manage to have varied basket-loads of fresh vegetables ready to be trucked to markets in Hong Kong daily. A good portion of the territory's garden land is concentrated near Yuen Long, Sek Kong and along the China border, as well as in scattered valleys and coastlines everywhere except on Hong Kong Island itself.

Left

Po Lin Monastery Of Hong Kong's more than 360 Chinese temples and monasteries, Po Lin on Lantau Island enjoys probably the most spectacular location, with Lantau Peak rising 934 metres in the background, and the monastery itself situated on Ngong Ping Plateau, 750 metres above sea level, on the northwestern side of Lantau. Construction of what will be the tallest statue of Buddha in Asia, standing 35 metres tall, has recently begun on the plateau.

Right

Po Lin Monastery Dedicated to the worship of Lord Buddha, Po Lin is a peaceful and friendly retreat where visitors can enjoy a vegetarian lunch in the dining hall, or even stay overnight — if they don't object to sleeping on hard boards in true monastic tradition. With an early start, it is also possible to scale Lantau Peak in time to watch the spectacular sunrise.

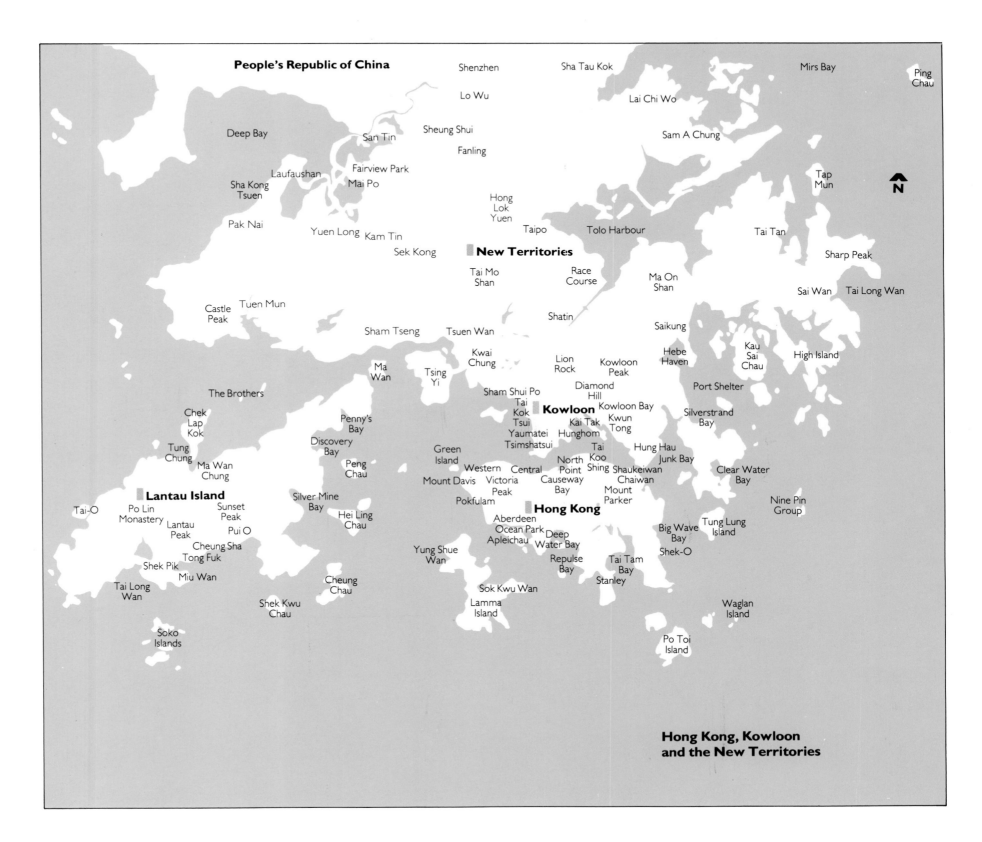

People's Republic of China

Shenzhen

Sha Tau Kok

Mirs Bay

Ping Chau

Lo Wu

Lai Chi Wo

Deep Bay

Sheung Shui

San Tin

Sam A Chung

Fanling

Fairview Park

Laufaushan

Tap Mun

Sha Kong Tsuen

Mai Po

Hong Lok Yuen

Pak Nai

Yuen Long

Kam Tin

Taipo

Tolo Harbour

Tai Tan

Sek Kong

New Territories

Sharp Peak

Tai Mo Shan

Race Course

Ma On Shan

Castle Peak

Tuen Mun

Sai Wan

Tai Long Wan

Shatin

Sham Tseng

Tsuen Wan

Saikung

Kwai Chung

Lion Rock

Kowloon Peak

Hebe Haven

Kau Sai Chau

High Island

Ma Wan

Tsing Yi

Diamond Hill

Port Shelter

The Brothers

Sham Shui Po

Tai Kok Tsui

Kowloon

Kowloon Bay

Kwun Tong

Silverstrand Bay

Chek Lap Kok

Penny's Bay

Kai Tak

Tung Chung

Discovery Bay

Yaumatei

Hunghom

Ma Wan Chung

Peng Chau

Green Island

Tsimshatsui

Tai Koo Shing

Hung Hau

Junk Bay

Western

Central

North Point

Shaukeiwan

Clear Water Bay

Lantau Island

Mount Davis

Victoria Peak

Causeway Bay

Chaiwan

Silver Mine Bay

Pokfulam

Mount Parker

Tai-O

Po Lin Monastery

Sunset Peak

Hei Ling Chau

Hong Kong

Nine Pin Group

Lantau Peak

Pui O

Aberdeen

Big Wave Bay

Tung Lung Island

Cheung Sha

Tong Fuk

Ocean Park

Apleichau

Deep Water Bay

Shek-O

Shek Pik

Miu Wan

Yung Shue Wan

Repulse Bay

Tai Tam Bay

Tai Long Wan

Cheung Chau

Stanley

Shek Kwu Chau

Sok Kwu Wan

Waglan Island

Soko Islands

Lamma Island

Po Toi Island

N

Hong Kong, Kowloon and the New Territories

139

INDEX

Preceding page
North Shore of Hong Kong Island, 1984 This photograph may seem quite up to date, at first glance. But look closely, because in even just a few years, Hong Kong has changed significantly. Since the signing of the Sino-British Joint Declaration at about the same time this photograph was taken, both local and international investment in Hong Kong have continued to make their impact on the skyline. (If you need some clues to find the changes, compare this picture to those on pages 12, 22, 23, 31 and 62).

Left
Yuen Long and Shenzhen Here is an odd contrast on the border between Hong Kong and China. The peaceful rural scene in the foreground is actually part of Yuen Long in Hong Kong's New Territories, while the modern cityscape behind is the Chinese border town of Shenzhen. The area has enjoyed explosive growth since it was declared a special economic zone in the late 70s. A dam which supplies Hong Kong with water is at top right and the square squat building, middle right, is the new border crossing facility.

Photography by:
Richard Strong Page 9
Robbie Shaw Pages 108, 109, 133
*Lew Roberts Pages 3, 6, 17, 47, 57, 59, 61, 72, 73, 90, 104, 113,
115, 116, 117, 122, 123, 128, 130, 132*
Magnus Bartlett Cover and all the other pictures

Central and Western Districts